Pillows of Promise

Neil and Kay Kennedy

8729 E 98th Place
Tulsa, Oklahoma 74133

pillowsofpromise.com

Foreword

"Praise the Lord, my soul; all my
inmost being, praise his holy name.
Praise the Lord, my soul,
and forget not all his benefits—
who forgives all your sins
and heals all your diseases."
Psalm 103:1-3 (NIV)

My grandfather, W.E. Smith, was a healing evangelist years before I was born. He would hold tent revivals and pray for the sick. He saw hundreds of people physically healed by the laying on of hands and prayer. I grew up hearing testimonies of miracles that he saw in his meetings. I knew that God could heal. I have always been intrigued by stories of people being healed. For most of my adult life, I have studied scriptures on healing and read many books on this subject.

Years ago, my mother had a pituitary tumor removed. Several years later, it began to grow back, and she needed treatment to hopefully make it shrink. God gave me the idea to make a pillow and embroider the word "Health" on the front because we were praying for my mother to regain her health. I created a hidden pocket in the back, and Neil and I put together a book with healing scriptures. I put the book in the pocket. Just like we read the Word of God and hide his promises in our hearts, the book is hidden in the pocket.

I gave the pillow to my mother, and she would read the scriptures and believe God was healing her. She went for 2 weeks of radiation every day. Around Christmastime, I would take her for her treatment, and afterward, we would go to lunch and shopping. She never got sick from the radiation and had plenty of energy to shop. The power of God was healing her. The tumor shrunk, and she lived another 15 years.

It is still God's will to heal people today. He hasn't changed his mind. This pillow is a reminder of his promises in his Word. I chose the word "Healed" for the front of this pillow because that is how Jesus sees us. He already paid for our healing on the cross; healing is included in our salvation; it was his idea. As you read the scriptures in this book, put your faith in Jesus and in what He said. He does not lie or change his mind (Numbers 23:19). Jesus didn't turn anyone away who came to him for healing.

Jesus said in Mark 11:22-23, "Have faith in God. For assuredly, I say to you, whoever says to this mountain, 'Be removed and be cast into the sea,' and does not doubt in his heart but believes that those things he says will be done, he will have whatever he says." Did you notice that the word "says" is used 3 times and the word "believes" is used only once? Is it possible that what you say is 3 times more important than what you believe? You can't speak to things you don't have authority over but have authority over your body. You can speak to your body, "Hip, be healed in Jesus' name!" "Migraine, get out in Jesus name!" Does this sound too simple? It's not; it works when we put our faith in Jesus. Begin to see yourself healed by the power of God inside you!

I pray that everyone who receives a pillow is encouraged, empowered by the Word of God, and inspired to take their healing. Keep the Word of God in your heart as you read this small book. Confess these scriptures out loud, declaring your healing and praising our God!

When you are healed, please email me your testimony at Kay@PillowsofPromise.com.
I would love to hear from you.

-Kay Kennedy

Desperation Causes Us To Reach

When you're desperate, you may become extreme. By this, I mean that you will go beyond the norm or what otherwise would have been limitations or comforts.

Sickness is the body operating in the extreme. It makes us uncomfortable and painful. Sickness constantly sends signals that something is very wrong with our bodies.

> *Hope deferred makes the heart sick,*
> *but a longing fulfilled is a tree of life.*
> *- Proverbs 13:12*

Sickness may cause you to sink into despair. Sickness, especially prolonged sickness, leads to a complete loss of hope.

The Bible reveals the desperation of a woman who had been hemorrhaging for twelve years.

Imagine the discomfort and pain of issuing blood for twelve years. To make matters worse, she spent all her wealth on the best medical care of the day, yet she did not get better; she grew worse. Now, she was sick and financially bankrupt. Compound that with being quarantined. Everyone considered her unclean. The Law demanded her isolation.

> ***When a woman has a discharge of blood for many days at a time other than her monthly period or has a discharge that continues beyond her period, she will be unclean as long as she has the discharge, just as in the days of her period. - Leviticus 15:25***

Recently, we know what isolation can do to people. The recent pandemic caused many people to give up hope and end their lives. Suicide rates soared during mandated isolation.

We also know that isolated confinement is one of the most severe punishments known to humanity. Isolated prisoners often lose their minds.

> ***Just then, a woman who had been subject to bleeding for twelve years came up behind him and touched the edge of his cloak. She said to herself, "If I only touch his cloak, I will be healed." - Matthew 9:20***

Luke tells us that this woman spent all of her money on physicians, and their best efforts were in vain.

What do you do when you're broke, hopeless, and bleeding?

You get desperate.

Desperation reaches.

She said to herself, "If I only touch his cloak, I will be healed."

When you're isolated, you do not have the option of others speaking for you. There are times when you must talk to yourself. The desperate woman said to herself, "If..."

IF

If is the supposition of or in the event of. If holds a promise, it plants a seed of hope. It is a unique promise— like the fine print in a contract. Something will occur in the event the opportunity appears.

She goes on to say, "If I only touch."

Now, she is reaching out. She is planning for the opportunity. When the opportunity arises, she will be ready.

What does she need to touch?

She says, "his cloak."

Knowing that she is unclean. Realizing she is quarantined, she knows she is breaking the Law.

She doesn't want to get his attention.

She doesn't want to beg.

She doesn't want Him even to know what she is doing.

The woman is simply desperate for healing. Desperation reaches.

> ***She came up behind him and touched the edge of his cloak, and immediately her bleeding stopped.***
> ***- Luke 8:44***

All she needed was a connection point. The fabric would be it. The moment that she touched the cloak, the hemorrhaging stopped. Twelve years of agony. Twelve years of isolation. Twelve years of rejection. Twelve years of loss.

Suddenly, she is healed.

"Who touched me?" Jesus asked.

This part of the account is so important. Jesus did not decide to heal her. He was unaware of her, passing by her, and didn't notice her.

So many people think that Jesus must decide for your healing. In reality, Jesus is healing!

This woman touched Jesus differently than those who were pressing against Him. They were not reaching for His virtue. They were not expecting a withdrawal from Him.

Jesus wanted to know, "Who touched me?"

> ***Jesus said, "Someone deliberately touched me, for I felt healing power go out from me." - Luke 8:46***

The woman made a withdrawal of healing power without Jesus making a decision.

Seeing that she could not hide it any longer, she confessed.

Then the woman, seeing that she could not go unnoticed, came trembling and fell at his feet. In the presence of all the people, she told why she had touched him and how she had been instantly healed.
- Luke 8:47

I want you to be encouraged by this exchange. So many do not receive healing because they disqualify themselves from the miracle. They consider themselves unworthy or unclean, not good enough, not deserving.

Now listen to Jesus' affirmation: "Daughter," he said to her, "your faith has made you well. Go in peace."

Who's faith?

Her faith. Jesus acknowledged her faith.

Faith is simply believing that God is true to His character. Faith in Jesus is believing that if you have seen Jesus, you have seen the Father's character.

God is not a man that He can lie. He is truthful. He has integrity.

This woman's faith inspired others to reach out of desperation to touch the fabric of His cloak.

> *When the people recognized Jesus, the news of his arrival spread quickly throughout the whole area, and soon people were bringing all their sick to be healed. They begged him to let the sick touch at least the fringe of his robe, and all who touched him were healed. - Matthew 14:35*

Where did all of these people get the idea that they could touch the cloak of Jesus and be healed?

They heard the report of the woman.

"Worship God! For the testimony of Jesus is the spirit of prophecy."
- Revelation 19:10

What God has done is what He will do. Amen means, "so be it."

When you hear the testimony of others and say, "Amen," you are saying, "Let it be done for me!"

Saying amen is affirming the omnipotence of God to act on your behalf. In other words, Jesus does not and cannot diminish His healing power. Another person's healing does not discredit you from receiving your healing. Some people disqualify themselves because they do not believe that they are worthy to receive anything from God. Well, that's where faith comes in.

Jesus is still healing people today. He is the same yesterday, today, and forever. If you are sick, don't give up hope. Reach out to Jesus in faith, and He will heal you.

God did extraordinary miracles through Paul so that even handkerchiefs and aprons that had touched him were taken to the sick, and their illnesses were cured, and the evil spirits left them. - Acts 19:11

God did not stop using cloths, handkerchiefs, and aprons. The Apostle Paul was also used in miraculous ways.

-Neil Kennedy

Healing Promises

My child, pay attention to what I say. Listen carefully to my words. Don't lose sight of them. Let them penetrate deep into your heart, for they bring life to those who find them, and healing to their whole body.

—Proverbs 4:20-22 NLT

He said, "If you listen carefully to the Lord your God and do what is right in his eyes, if you pay attention to his commands and keep all his decrees, I will not bring on you any of the diseases I brought on the Egyptians, "for I am the Lord who heals you."

—Exodus 15:26 NLT

Massive crowds followed him and
he healed all who were sick.

—Matthew 19:2 TPT

They had come to hear him and to be healed of their diseases; and those troubled by evil spirits were healed.

—Luke 6:18 NLT

He brought them forth also with silver and gold: And there was not one feeble person among their tribes.

—*Psalm 105:37*

Instantly the leprosy disappeared, and the man was healed.

—Mark 1:42 NLT

But he was wounded for our
transgressions, he was bruised for our
iniquities: the chastisement of our
peace was upon him; and
with his stripes we are healed.

—*Isaiah 53:5 KJV*

He sent out his word and healed them,
snatching them from the door of death.

—Psalm 107:20 NLT

For she kept saying to herself, "If I could only touch his prayer shawl I would be healed."

—Matthew 9:21 TPT

Jesus turned around, and when he saw her he said, "Daughter, be encouraged! Your faith has made you well." And the woman was healed at that moment.

—Matthew 9:22 NLT

The blind and the lame came to him in the Temple, and he healed them.

—*Matthew 21:14 NLT*

Moved with compassion, Jesus reached out and touched him. "I am willing," he said. "Be healed!" Instantly the leprosy disappeared, and the man was healed.

—Mark 1:41-42 NLT

And they cast out many demons and healed many sick people, anointing them with olive oil.

—Mark 6:13 NLT

Everyone tried to touch him, because healing power went out from him, and he healed everyone.

—Luke 6:19 NLT

And Jesus said to the man, "Stand up and go. Your faith has healed you."

—Luke 17:19 NLT

"What do you want me to do for you?" "Lord," he said, "I want to see!" And Jesus said, "All right, receive your sight! Your faith has healed you." Instantly the man could see, and he followed Jesus, praising God. And all who saw it praised God, too.

—*Luke 18:42-43 NLT*

Then all the other sick people on the island came and were healed.

—Acts 28:9 NLT

Through faith in the name of Jesus, this man was healed—and you know how crippled he was before. Faith in Jesus' name has healed him before your very eyes.

—*Acts 3:16 NLT*

Confess your sins to each other and pray for each other so that you may be healed. The earnest prayer of a righteous person has great power and produces wonderful results.

—James 5:16 NLT

Then Abraham prayed to God, and God healed Abimelech, his wife, and his female servants, so they could have children.

—Genesis 20:17 NLT

O Lord, my healing God, I cried out for a miracle and you healed me!

—Psalms 30:2 TPT

Jesus reached out and touched him. "I am willing," he said. "Be healed!" And instantly the leprosy disappeared.

—Matthew 8:3 NLT

"Dear woman," Jesus said to her, "your faith is great. Your request is granted." And her daughter was instantly healed.

—Matthew 15:28 NLT

He had healed many people that day,
so all the sick people eagerly pushed
forward to touch him.

—*Mark 3:10 NLT*

For she thought to herself, "If I can just touch his robe, I will be healed." Immediately the bleeding stopped, and she could feel in her body that she had been healed of her terrible condition.

—Mark 5:28-29 NLT

When Jesus saw her, he called her over and said, “Dear woman, you are healed of your sickness!”

—Luke 13:12 NLT

Jesus asked the Pharisees and experts in religious law, "Is it permitted in the law to heal people on the Sabbath day, or not?" When they refused to answer, Jesus touched the sick man and healed him and sent him away.

—Luke 14:3-4 NLT

One of them, when he saw that he was healed, came back to Jesus, shouting, "Praise God!"

—Luke 15:15 NLT

A huge crowd kept following him
wherever he went, because they saw his
miraculous signs as he healed the sick.

—John 6:2 NLT

Jesus traveled throughout the region of Galilee, teaching in the synagogues and announcing the Good News about the Kingdom. And he healed every kind of disease and illness.

—*Matthew 4:23 NLT*

Then Jesus said to the Roman officer, "Go back home. Because you believed, it has happened." And the young servant was healed that same hour.

—*Matthew 8:13 NLT*

That evening many demon-possessed people were brought to Jesus. He cast out the evil spirits with a simple command, and he healed all the sick.

—*Matthew 8:16 NLT*

Jesus turned around, and when he saw her he said, "Daughter, be encouraged! Your faith has made you well." And the woman was healed at that moment.

—Matthew 9:22 NLT

But Jesus knew what they were planning. So he left that area, and many people followed him. He healed all the sick among them.

—Matthew 12:15 NLT

Then a demon-possessed man, who was blind and couldn't speak, was brought to Jesus. He healed the man so that he could both speak and see.

—Matthew 12:22 NLT

Jesus saw the huge crowd as he stepped from the boat, and he had compassion on them and healed their sick.

—Matthew 14:14 NLT

When the people recognized Jesus,
the news of his arrival spread quickly
throughout the whole area, and soon
people were bringing all their
sick to be healed.

—Matthew 14:35 NLT

They begged him to let the sick touch at least the fringe of his robe, and all who touched him were healed.

—Matthew 14:36 NLT

And Jesus said to him, "Go, for your faith has healed you." Instantly the man could see, and he followed Jesus down the road.

—Mark 10:52 NLT

But despite Jesus' instructions, the report of his power spread even faster, and vast crowds came to hear him preach and to be healed of their diseases.

—Luke 5:15 NLT

Jesus told him, "Stand up, pick up your mat, and walk!" Instantly, the man was healed! He rolled up his sleeping mat and began walking! But this miracle happened on the Sabbath.

—John 5:8-9 NLT

Then Peter took the lame man by the right hand and helped him up. And as he did, the man's feet and ankles were instantly healed and strengthened. He jumped up, stood on his feet, and began to walk! Then, walking, leaping, and praising God, he went into the Temple with them.

—Acts 3:7-8 NLT

So Naaman went down to the Jordan River and dipped himself seven times, as the man of God had instructed him. And his skin became as healthy as the skin of a young child, and he was healed!

—2 Kings 5:14 NLT

Many evil spirits were cast out,
screaming as they left their victims.
And many who had been paralyzed or
lame were healed.

—*Acts 8:7 NLT*

Peter said to him, "Aeneas, Jesus Christ heals you! Get up, and roll up your sleeping mat!" And he was healed instantly.

—*Acts 9:34 NLT*

God did extraordinary miracles
through Paul, so that even
handkerchiefs and aprons that had
touched him were taken to the sick,
and their illnesses were cured and the
evil spirits left them.

—Acts 19:11-12 NIV

Crowds came from the villages around Jerusalem, bringing their sick and those possessed by evil spirits, and they were all healed.

—Acts 5:16 NLT

News about him spread as far as Syria, and people soon began bringing to him all who were sick. And whatever their sickness or disease, or if they were demon possessed or epileptic or paralyzed—he healed them all.

—Matthew 4:24 NLT

Jesus traveled through all the towns and villages of that area, teaching in the synagogues and announcing the Good News about the Kingdom. And he healed every kind of disease and illness.

—Matthew 9:35 NLT

A vast crowd brought to him people who were lame, blind, crippled, those who couldn't speak, and many others. They laid them before Jesus, and he healed them all.

—Matthew 15:30 NLT

Wherever he went—in villages, cities, or the countryside—they brought the sick out to the marketplaces. They begged him to let the sick touch at least the fringe of his robe, and all who touched him were healed.

—*Mark 6:56 NLT*

As the sun went down that evening, people throughout the village brought sick family members to Jesus. No matter what their diseases were, the touch of his hand healed every one.

—Luke 4:40 NLT

But the crowds found out where he was going, and they followed him. He welcomed them and taught them about the Kingdom of God, and he healed those who were sick.

—Luke 9:11 NLT

As the boy came forward, the demon knocked him to the ground and threw him into a violent convulsion. But Jesus rebuked the evil spirit and healed the boy. Then he gave him back to his father.

—*Luke 9:42*

Let me clearly state to all of you and to all the people of Israel that he was healed by the powerful name of Jesus Christ the Nazarene, the man you crucified but whom God raised from the dead.

—*Acts 4:10 NLT*

Who his own self bare our sins in his own body on the tree, that we, being dead to sins, should live unto righteousness: by whose stripes ye were healed.

—1 Peter 2:24 KJV

Jesus reached out and touched him. "I am willing," he said. "Be healed!" And instantly the leprosy disappeared.

—Luke 5:13 NLT

When the woman realized that she could not stay hidden, she began to tremble and fell to her knees in front of him. The whole crowd heard her explain why she had touched him and that she had been immediately healed.

—Luke 8:47 NLT

And he said unto her, Daughter, be of good comfort: thy faith hath made thee whole; go in peace.

—*Luke 8:48 KJV*

He heals the brokenhearted and
bandages their wounds.

—Psalm 147:3 NLT

Jesus said,
"I will come and heal him."
—Matthew 8:7 NLT

He forgives all my sins and
heals all my diseases.

—Psalm 103:3 NIV

When they are sick, lying upon their bed of suffering, God will restore them. He will raise them up again and restore them back to health.

—*Psalm 41:3 NLT*

Think of it—the Lord is ready to heal me! I will sing his praises with instruments every day of my life in the Temple of the Lord.

—Isaiah 38:20 NLT

O Lord, if you heal me, I will be truly healed; if you save me, I will be truly saved. My praises are for you alone!

—Jeremiah 17:14 NLT

"I will give you back your health and heal your wounds," says the Lord. "For you are called an outcast— Jerusalem for whom no one cares."

—Jeremiah 30:17 NLT

Jesus called his twelve disciples together and gave them authority to cast out evil spirits and to heal every kind of disease and illness.

—*Matthew 10:1 NLT*

Therefore, strengthen your feeble arms and weak knees. "Make level paths for your feet," so that the lame may not be disabled, but rather healed.

—Hebrews 12:12-13

At that very time, Jesus cured many people of their diseases, illnesses, and evil spirits, and he restored sight to many who were blind.

—Luke 7:21 NLT

He gives power to the weak and
strength to the powerless.
—Isaiah 40:29 NLT

And he said to her, "Daughter, your faith has made you well. Go in peace. Your suffering is over."

—*Mark 5:34 NLT*

With long life I will satisfy him and
show him my salvation.

—Psalm 91:16 NIV

I will not die; instead, I will live to
tell what the Lord has done.

—Psalm 118:17 NLT

For with God nothing
will be impossible.

—Luke 1:37 NKJV

For with God nothing is ever
impossible and no word from God
shall be without power or
impossible of fulfillment.

—Luke 1:37 AMPC

And blessed is she that believed: for there shall be a performance of those things which were told her from the Lord.

—Luke 1:45 KJV

Jesus responded, "What appears humanly impossible is more than possible with God. For God can do what man cannot."

—Luke 18:27 TPT

For God has not given us a spirit of fear; but of power, and of love, and of a sound mind."

—2 Timothy 1:7 KJV

"If you can?" said Jesus. "Everything
is possible for one who believes."
Immediately the boy's father exclaimed,
"I do believe; help me overcome
my unbelief!"

—Mark 9:23-24 NIV

I also pray that you will understand the incredible greatness of God's power for us who believe him. This is the same mighty power that raised Christ from the dead and seated him in the place of honor at God's right hand in the heavenly realms.

—Ephesians 1:19-20 NLT

He replied, "Because you have so little faith. Truly I tell you, if you have faith as small as a mustard seed, you can say to this mountain, 'Move from here to there,' and it will move. Nothing will be impossible for you."

—*Matthew 17:20 NIV*

God can do anything, you know—far more than you could ever imagine or guess or request in your wildest dreams! He does it not by pushing us around but by working within us, his Spirit deeply and gently within us.

—Ephesians 3:20-21 MSG

So Jesus answered and said to them, "Have faith in God. For assuredly, I say to you, whoever says to this mountain, 'Be removed and be cast into the sea,' and does not doubt in his heart, but believes that those things he says will be done, he will have whatever he says.

—Mark 11:22-23 NKJV

Therefore I say to you, whatever things you ask when you pray, believe that you receive them, and you will have them.

—Mark 11:24 NKJV

Jesus Christ is the same
yesterday, today, and forever.

—Hebrews 13:8 NLT

Never stop praying.

—1 Thessalonians 5:17